IF CATS COULD TALK!

IF CATS COULD TALK!

BY
P. C. VEY

Ⓟ
A PLUME BOOK

PLUME
Published by the Penguin Group
Penguin Books USA Inc., 375 Hudson Street, New York, New York 10014, U.S.A.
Penguin Books Ltd, 27 Wrights Lane, London W8 5TZ, England
Penguin Books Australia Ltd, Ringwood, Victoria, Australia
Penguin Books Canada Ltd, 2801 John Street, Markham, Ontario, Canada L3R 1B4
Penguin Books (N.Z.) Ltd, 182–190 Wairau Road, Auckland 10, New Zealand

Penguin Books Ltd, Registered Offices: Harmondsworth, Middlesex, England

First published by Plume, an imprint of
New American Library, a division of Penguin Books USA Inc.

First Printing, July, 1991
10 9 8 7 6 5 4 3 2 1

Some cartoons in this collection appeared previously in *New Woman*,
Redbook, *Men's Life*, and *Cosmopolitan*.

LIBRARY OF CONGRESS CATALOGING-IN-PUBLICATION DATA

Vey, P. C. (Peter C.)
    If cats could talk! / by P.C. Vey.
        p.   cm.
    ISBN 0-452-26642-4
    1. Cats—Caricatures and cartoons.   2. American wit and humor,
Pictorial.   I. Title.
NC1429.V57A4   1991
741.5'973—dc20
                                                                    90-25476
                                                                         CIP

Printed in the United States of America

BOOKS ARE AVAILABLE AT QUANTITY DISCOUNTS WHEN USED TO PROMOTE PRODUCTS OR SERVICES. FOR
INFORMATION PLEASE WRITE TO PREMIUM MARKETING DIVISION, PENGUIN BOOKS INC., 375 HUDSON
STREET, NEW YORK, NEW YORK 10014.

"Now that the kids are grown and out on their own, it would be nice if you invited me to sit at the table once in a while."

P. C. VEY

"Ever notice how their eyes seem to follow you around the room?"

P.C.VEY

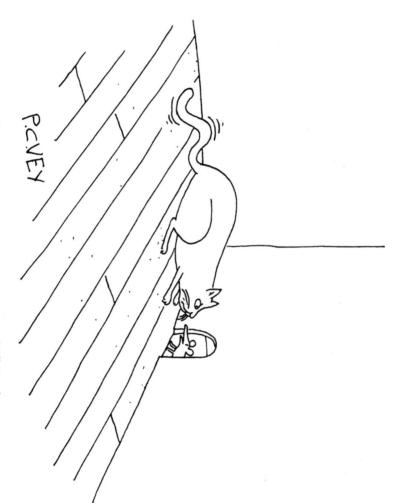

"Tell you what, you leave me alone, and I'll teach you how to use a can opener."

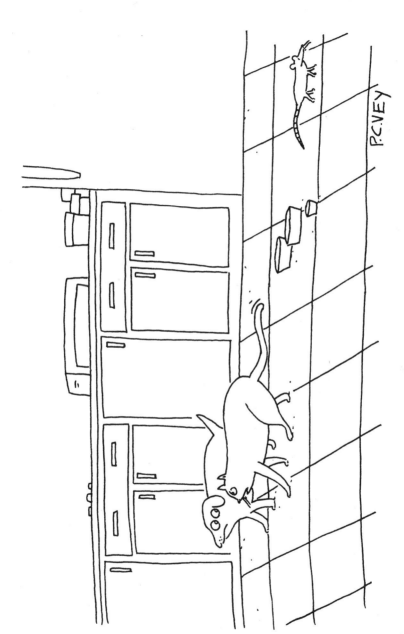

"If you ask me, things are getting a little too liberal around here."

P.C.VEY

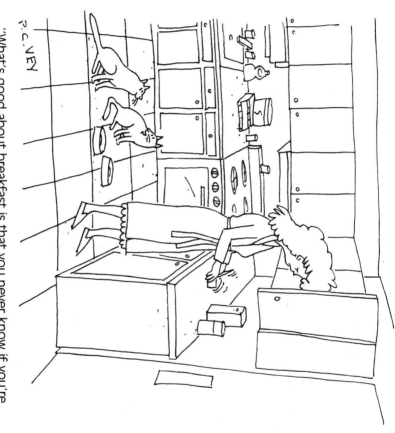

"What's good about breakfast is that you never know if you're going to get cat food or chunk white tuna in spring water."

P.C.VEY

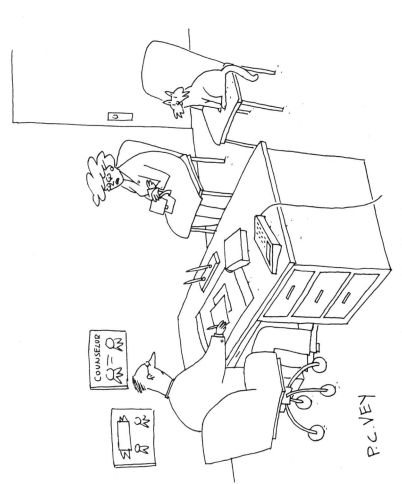

"And then my husband said, 'Either that cat goes, or I go.'"

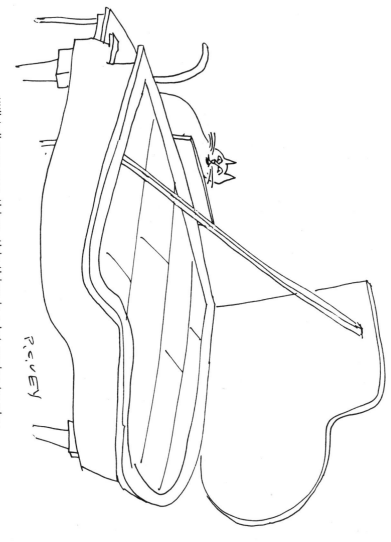

"I'll tell you one thing, this thing is a lot easier to play since I was declawed."

"Well, I thought the meal was delicious . . . all except for the 'Kittybitts' at the end of the course."

P.C.VEY

"And now, for fifty thousand dollars, what are the first three ingredients of 'Kittybitts Cat Food's Surprise Dinner'?"

"This had better be good."

P.C.VEY

"Fourteen mice in trouble . . . and here with that story. . . ."

P.C. VEY

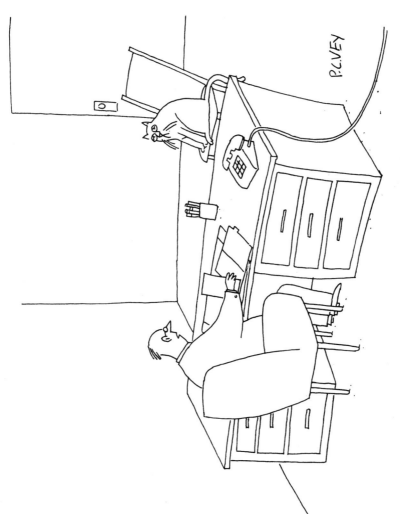

"Frankly, we were looking for someone who isn't a cat."

"Did you know that sweat, sun, seawater, and chlorine can wreak havoc with your hair?"

P.C. VEY

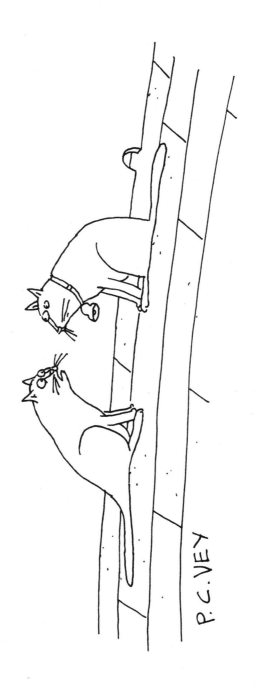

"I tried the bell diet once, but I couldn't stand the mice laughing at me."

P.C. VEY

"Did you feed the cat today?"

P.C.VEY

"Next."

"I hope you don't talk about me when I'm out."

P.C.VEV

"I know it's illegal, but frankly, we just couldn't get by without the cash and jewelry he brings home every night."

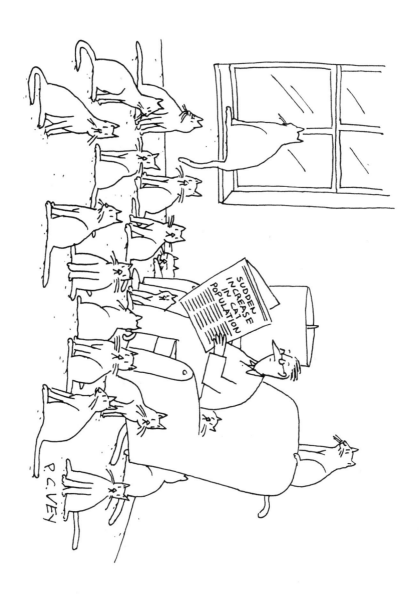

"Do you believe that cat of theirs? It seemed like he'd do
anything to get out of that apartment."

P.C.VEY

"She's an outdoors cat."

P.C.VEY

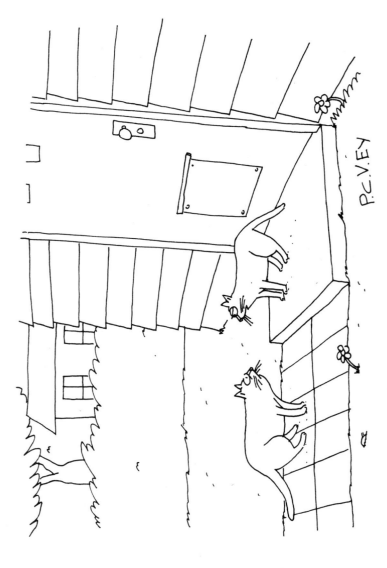

P.C.VEY

"I had a wonderful time, but I never mate on the first date."

P.C.VEY

"It's your cat, Mr. Phillips. She wants to know why you neglected to pet her on your way out of the house this morning."

"Damn! Which one is the mouseburger?"

P.C. VEY

"Hey, Harry, how old is seven in cat years?"

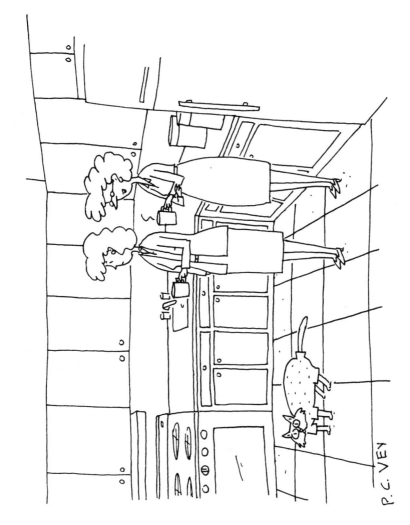

"I had it made from all his fur balls."

P.C. VEY

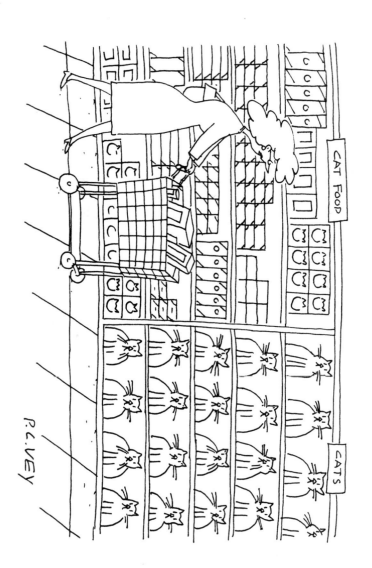

"Normally I would never impose on your sleep like this, but seeing how there's a large man with a ski mask over his head making a mess downstairs, I thought I'd make an exception."

P.C. VEY

P. C. VEY

" . . . And one final question: Do the people you live with
know you feel this way about them?"

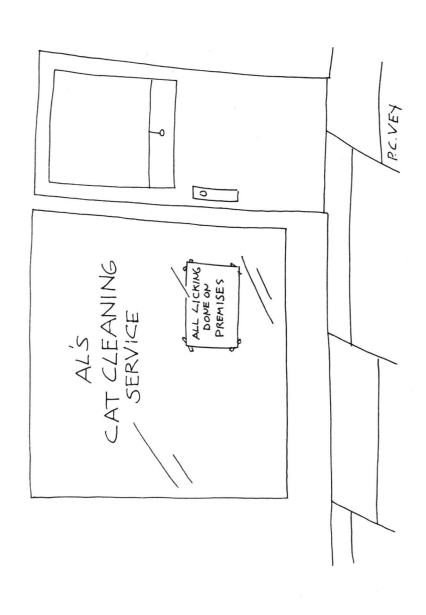

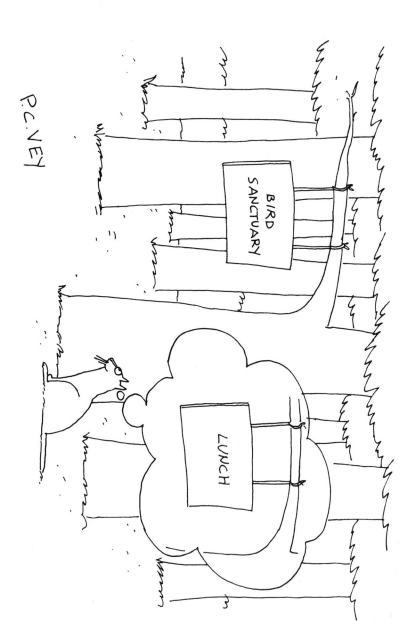

"Of course it's no fun. This is a dog toy."

"Hey, listen, Frank, I gotta go. The cat's acting like a dog again."

"She's allergic to people."

P.C.VEY

"Marry me, Doris. Your cat will never know."

"... And now voted Most Likely to Chase a Squirrel Up a Forty-Foot Tree and Not Be Able to Come Down for Two Days."

P.C.VEY

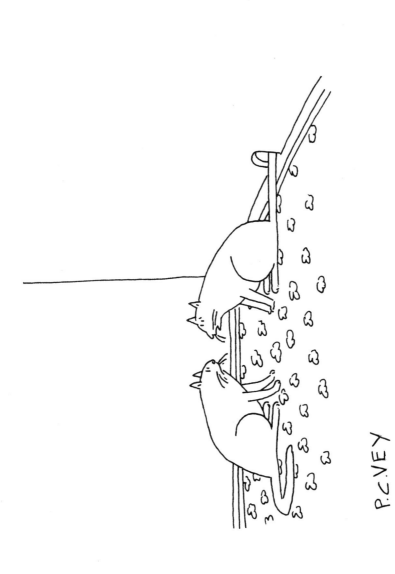

"My tail hurts."

P.C.VEY

"Whatever you do, don't ask about Kitty's fur-ball collection."

"Well, no, he doesn't have an appointment, but he thought that since you took the time to pet him outside the coffee shop this morning you wouldn't mind seeing him again."

"Now that we've moved to the eighty-second floor, Kitty doesn't like to sit on the windowsill anymore."

"Honestly! Sometimes I think you like that cat more than you like me!"

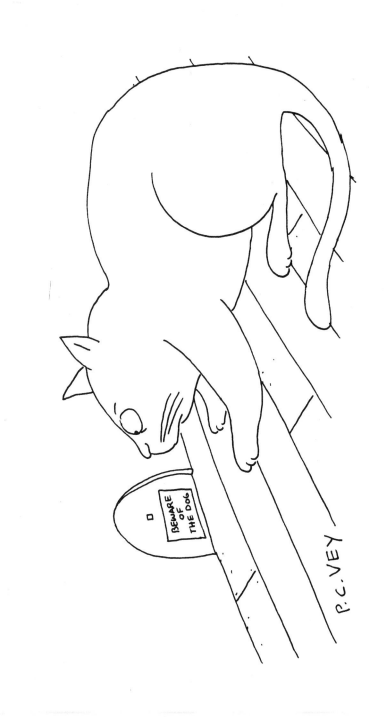

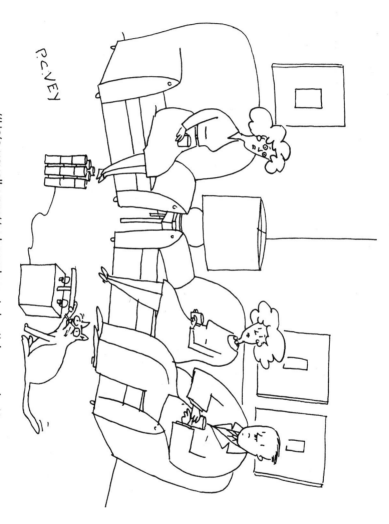

"He's usually pretty harmless. I don't know what's got into him now."

P.C.VEY

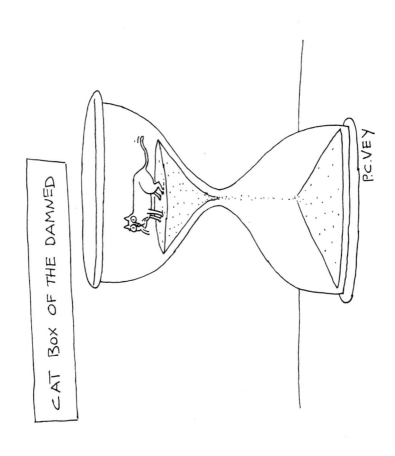

CAT BOX OF THE DAMNED

P.C. VEY

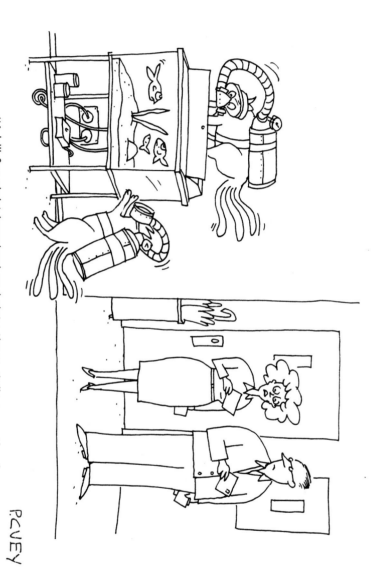

"A bill for eight hundred and sixty-three dollars worth of scuba equipment?! Honey, did you buy eight hundred and sixty-three dollars worth of scuba equipment?!"

PEVEY

"Well, wouldn't you know it. He has the all tropical fish and small bird channel on again."

P.C.VEY

"Okay, Binky, would you mind watching this thing
while I go see if I can find some butter and garlic?"

P.C. VEY

"I liked ripping the house plants to shreds better."

P.C. VEY

P.C. VEY

"Let's not play games. It's turkey with giblets and gravy you're after, not me!"

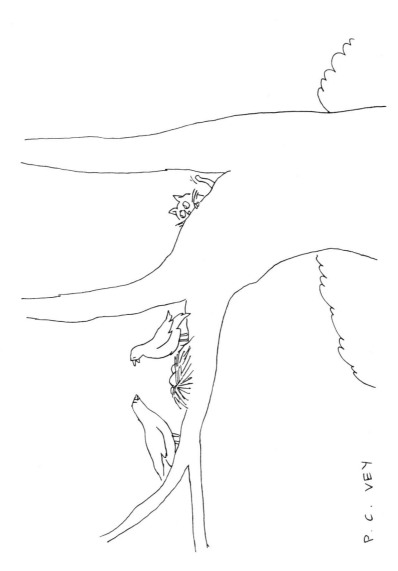

"That cat's pretty stupid. Next thing you know, he'll get himself caught in a tree."

P. C. VEY

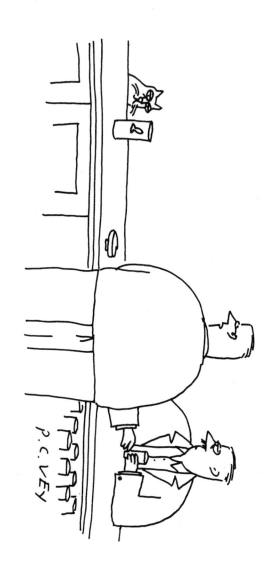

"It's a pretty good drink . . . . if you don't mind the fish-flavored Kitty Treat."

CAT-O-NINE TAILS

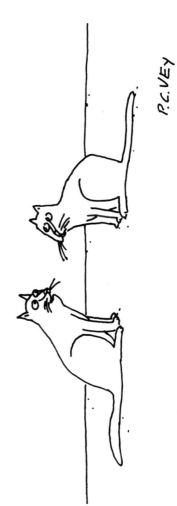

"I left the other eight at home."

P.C. VEY

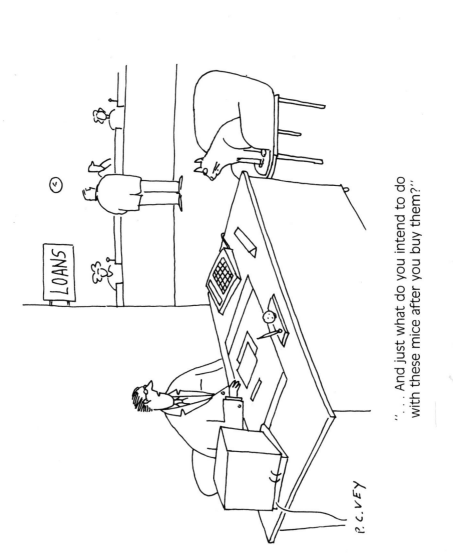

" . . . And just what do you intend to do with these mice after you buy them?"

P.C. VEY

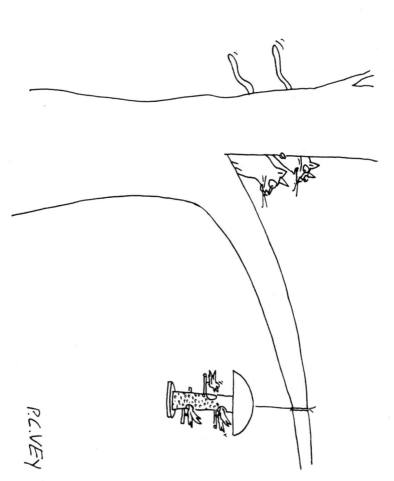

"Not only are they better tasting than canned food, but they come with stuffing."

P.C. VEY

"Prescription-strength catnip? Gee, I don't know, I'll have to take a look."

"I don't mean to intrude, but I grew up in this house and I'd just like to come in and see if the old territorial markings are still intact."

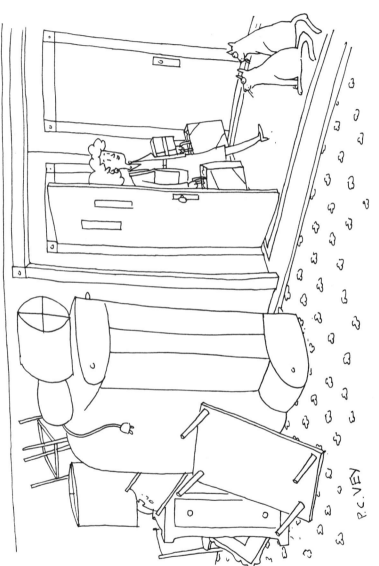

"And how did you keep yourself busy while I was out?"

P.C. VEY

"The ball of yarn was an increasing source of annoyance to Tom, and soon something would have to be done about it."

POVEY

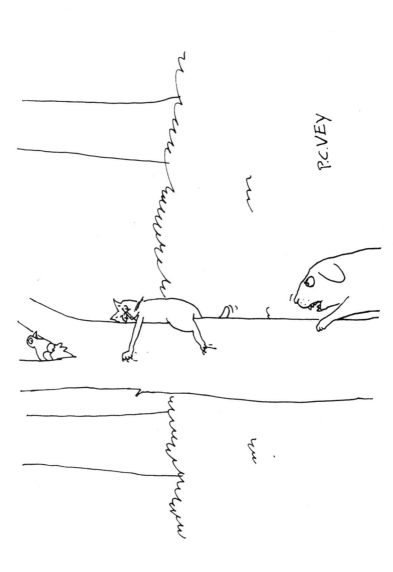

P.C.VEY

Binky discovers the food chain.

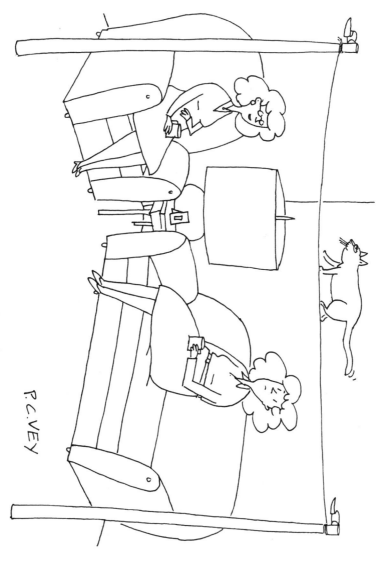

"Agile little creature, isn't she?"

P.C.VEY

P.C. VEY

"Would you like me to clean that window?"

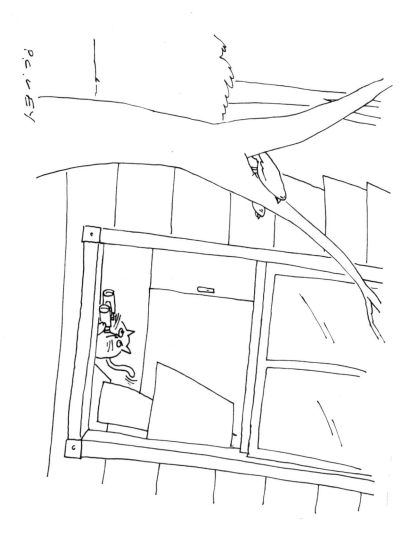

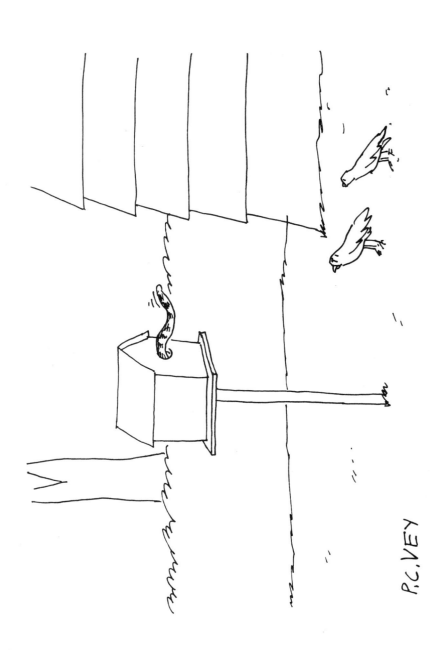

P.C.VEY

"Now, aren't you sorry you wondered where your food came from?"

P.C.VEY

P.C. VEY

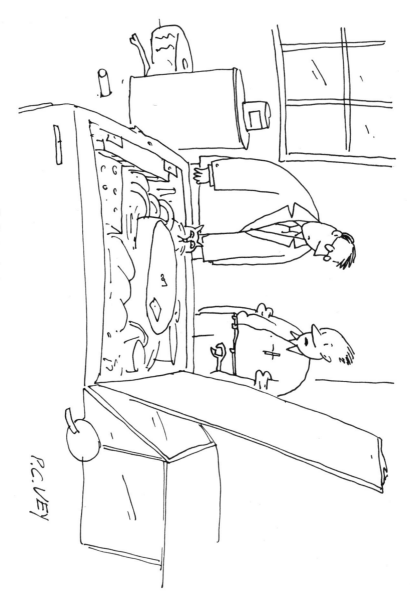

"Well, first of all, I'd get rid of that cat."

P.C. VEY

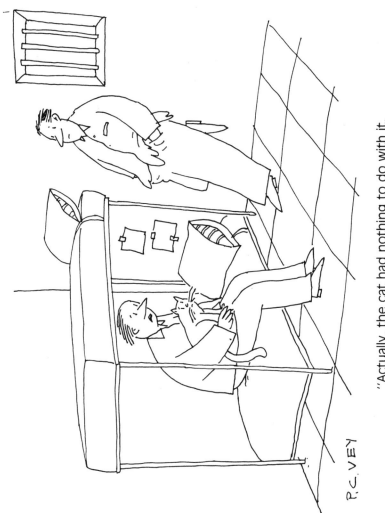

"Actually, the cat had nothing to do with it,
but the judge wouldn't believe me."

P.C. VEY

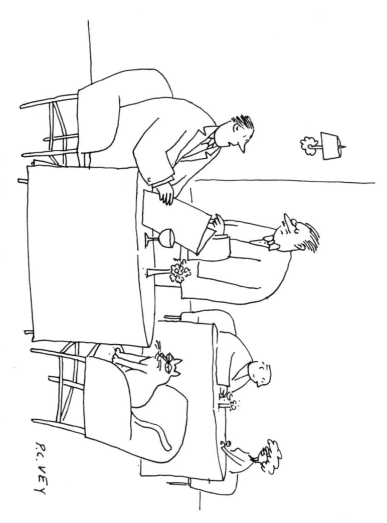

"... And the cat will have a can of cat food."

P.C. VEY

"You can get rid of that bell now."

P.C. VEY

"Kind of looks like the same mouse I left in her bed last week."

P.C. VEY

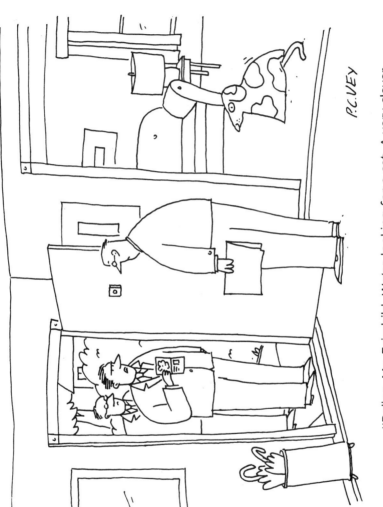

"Police, Mr. Fairchild. We're looking for a cat. A very clever cat. A cat that's been disguising himself as a dog."

P.C.VEY

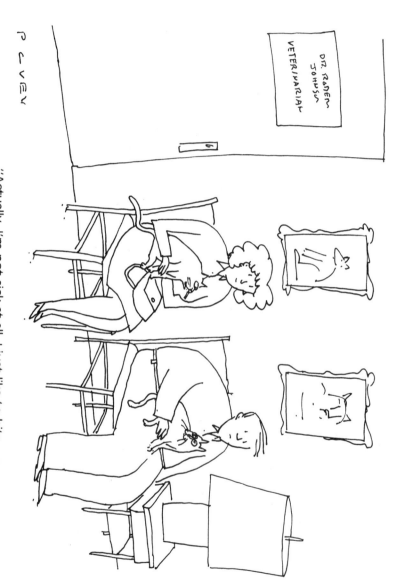

"Actually, I'm not sick at all, I just like to bite and scratch the doctor when he gives me that pill."

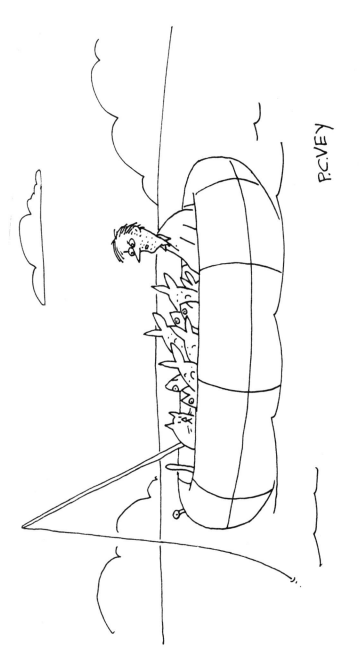

P.C.VEY

"Okay! Okay! So you can catch fish! Let's see how good you are at keeping those claws contracted!!"

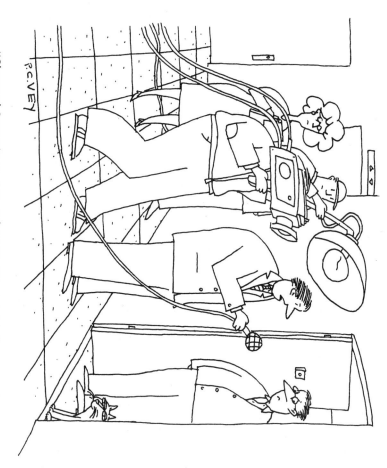

"Channel Seventeen, Mr. Johnson. Your cat tells us you've switched to the cheaper brand of cat food. Do you have a comment?"

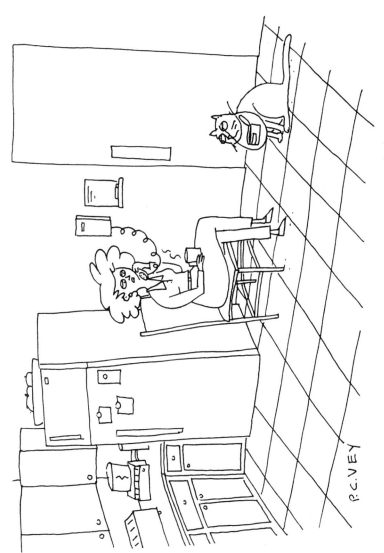

"Got to go now, Doris. Kitty wants to get fed."

P.C.VEY

"It's a great idea, but frankly we just don't think there's a market for a novel about a cat that can not only read and write, but uses a word processor as well."

P.C.VEY

"Doris, call my wife and ask her if the Wilson report is in the cat's basket."

"His is a sad story, Elizabeth, much like my own."

And then he suddenly realized she was reading about cats in general and not him in particular.

P.C.VEY

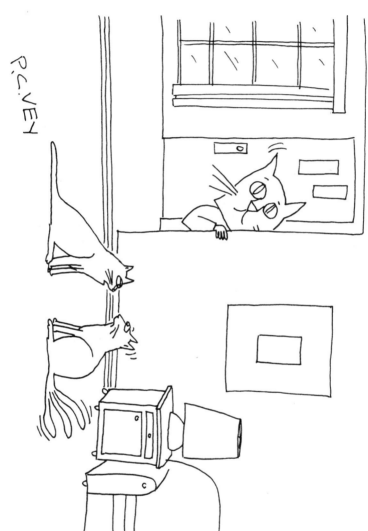

"Ignore him. He's just trying to freak us out."

P.C.VEY

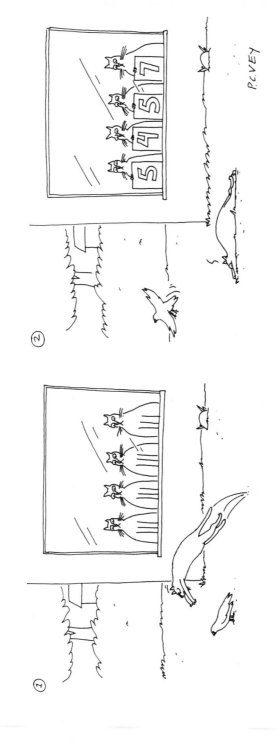

PL VEY

"I just thought you would like to know that those new tear-proof plastic bags you put the scraps in after dinner are not as tear-proof as you would imagine."

"I suppose I should have told you I'm allergic to cats."

"Very unusual case. Most tails don't fight back after being chased."

P.C. VEY

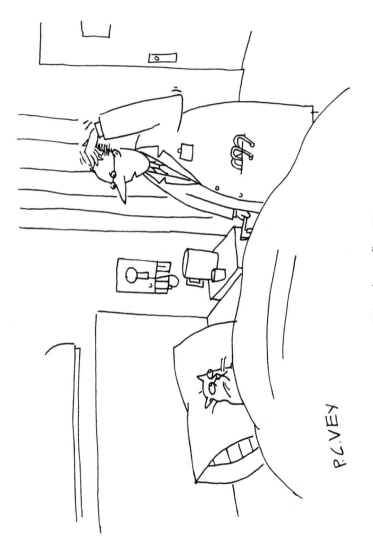

P.C.VEY

"You have fleas!"

"Okay, you got him here, and he's enjoying himself, but you still haven't gotten him in the water."

Plume

LAUGH ALONG WITH PLUME

☐ **THE SECRET LIFE OF DOGS** *Cartoons* by David Sipress. Howl with laughter as this outrageous cartoonist probes the deep recesses of the canine mind.
(264944—$5.95)

☐ **WHAT ARE THE CHANCES?** *Risks, Odds, and Likelihood in Everyday Life* by **Bernard Siskin and Jerome Staller with David Rorvik.** Chances are this fascinating, funny, and addictive compendium of trivia will have readers clamoring for more.
(265088—$7.95)

☐ **CALVES CAN BE SO CRUEL** *The Best of Rubes Cartoons* by **Leigh Rubin.** Hilarious cartoons about the wild kingdom (both animal and human) by the nationally syndicated ceator of Rubes.
(265096—$5.95)

☐ **MORE NEWS OF THE WEIRD** by Chuck Sheperd, **John J. Kohut & Roland Sweet.** Gathered here in one hilarious volume are more than 500 of the weirdest, craziest, most outlandish stories ever to find their way into our nation's newspapers.
(265452—$7.95)

☐ **DR. KOOKIE, YOU'RE RIGHT!** by **Mike Royko.** Another bestselling and uproarious collection of columns from the nationally syndicated Pulitzer Prize-winner. "Exuberantly cynical, this is vintage Royko."—*Publishers Weekly*
(265150—$8.95)

Prices slightly higher in Canada.

Buy them at your local bookstore or use this convenient coupon for ordering.

NEW AMERICAN LIBRARY
P.O. Box 999, Bergenfield, New Jersey 07621

Please send me the books I have checked above. I am enclosing $_____ (please add
$1.50 to this order to cover postage and handling). Send check or money order—no cash or C.O.D.'s.
Prices and numbers are subject to change without notice.

Name _____

Address _____

City _____ State _____ Zip Code _____

Allow 4-6 weeks for delivery.
This offer is subject to withdrawal without notice.